Practice Guidebook for Object Oriented C++ Language

S.ANBAZHAGAN

ISBN: 1540761517
ISBN-13: 978-1540761514

DEDICATION

This book is dedicated to the lotus feet of THE MOTHER & SRI AUROBINDO.

CONTENTS

ACKNOWLEDGMENTS

First and foremost, I sincerely record my gratitude to god almighty for having bestowed this opportunity on me and extending his grace to complete this book successfully.

I am especially blessed in getting the support of my well-wisher and philosopher, Mrs. Rama Srinivasan, Besant Nagar, Chennai. Without her magnanimous assistance in my academics, I would not have been able to achieve this opportunity. She has been the beacon light in rendering timely moral support.

I am thankful to my colleagues and the students for all their help. I am grateful to wife Mrs.N.Nalini Anbazhagan, my mother Mrs.S.Chandra Swaminathan, sons A.Anish and A.Akhil for having cooperated with me to complete this book. It was the inspiration that I got from them which helped me to mold this work. I thank all my family members, parents-in-law, friends and other well-wishers for their interest in my success.

Finally, I express my sincere thanks to all the CreateSpace members, for his guidance in every step. His significant cooperation and valuable suggestions provided a strong ground for this book. Without his continuous interest and support, this book could not have been completed successfully.

1 BASIC PROGRAMS

1. Program to print the words "My first program in C++"

```cpp
#include <iostream.h>
void main()
{
    cout<<"\nMy first program in C++";
}
```

2. Program to print the amount and (x,y) coordinate values using standard output stream object

```cpp
#include <iostream.h>
void main()
{
    float amt=6.5;
    int x=34,y=23;
    cout<<"\nAmount = Rs. "<<amt;
    cout<<"\n("<<x<<","<<y<<")";
}
```

3. Program to read & print the age and height of the person

```cpp
#include <iostream.h>
void main()
{
    int age;
    float ht;
    cout<<"\nEnter age: ";
    cin>>age;
    cout<<"\nEnter height: ";
    cin>>ht;
    cout<<"\nAge is "<<age;
    cout<<"\nHeight is "<<ht;
}
```

4. Program to calculate the area & circumference of the circle

```cpp
#include <iostream.h>
#define PI 3.14
void main()
{
    float r, a, c;
    cout<<"\nEnter radius: ";
    cin>>r;
    a = PI * r * r;
    c = 2 * PI * r;
    cout<<"Radius is "<<r;
    cout<<"\nArea is "<<a<<"\nCircumference is "<<c;
}
```

5. Program to calculate the area & perimeter of the rectangle

```cpp
#include <iostream.h>
void main()
{
    float l, b, a, p;
    cout<<"\nEnter length & breadth\n";
    cin>>l>>b;
    a = l * b;
    p = 2 * (l + b);
    cout<<"\nLength is "<<l<<"\nBreadth is "<<b;
    cout<<"\nArea is "<<a<<"\nPerimeter is "<<p;
}
```

6. Program to calculate the simple interest

```cpp
#include <iostream.h>
void main()
{
    float p, n, r, si;
    cout<<"\nEnter principle amount, number of year and rate of interest\n";
    cin>>p>>n>>r;
    si = p * n * r / 100;
    cout<<"\nPrinciple amount is "<<p;
    cout<<"\nNumber of year is "<<n;
    cout<<"\nRate of interest is "<<r;
    cout<<"\nSimple interest is "<<si;
}
```

7. Program to understand the type casting

```cpp
#include <iostream.h>
void main()
{
    int a = 10, b = 3;
    float r;
    r = a / b;
```

```cpp
        cout<<"\nResult is "<<r;
        r = a / float(b);
        cout<<"\nResult is "<<r;
        r = float(a) / b;
        cout<<"\nResult is "<<r;
}
```

8. Program to convert temperature in Celsius to Fahrenheit

```cpp
#include <iostream.h>
void main()
{
        float c, f;
        cout<<"\nEnter temperature in Celsius: ";
        cin>>c;
        f = 9 / 5.0 * c + 32;
        cout<<"\nTemperature in Fahrenheit is "<<f;
}
```

9. Program to find the square root of the given number

```cpp
#include <iostream.h>
#include <math.h>
void main()
{
        double n, r;
        cout<<"\nEnter number: ";
        cin>>n;
        r = sqrt(n);
        cout<<"Square root of "<<n<<" is "<<r;
}
```

10. Program to understand the concept of Reference variable

```cpp
#include <iostream.h>
void main()
{
        int oldVar = 10;
        int &newVar = oldVar;
        cout<<"\nOld variable is "<<oldVar;
        cout<<"\nNew variable is "<<newVar;
        newVar = 100;
        cout<<"\nOld variable is "<<oldVar;
        cout<<"\nNew variable is "<<newVar;
}
```

2 C++ FUNCTION PROGRAMS

1. Program to understand the concepts of function

```cpp
// Method 1
#include <iostream.h>
void printmyname();  /* Function Declaration */
void main()
{
    printmyname();  /* Calling Function */
    printmyname();
    printmyname();
}
                        /* Called Function */
void printmyname()   /* Function Definition */
{
    cout<<"\nBjarne Stroustrup";
}
```

```cpp
// Method 2
#include <iostream.h>
                        /* Called Function */
void printmyname()   /* Function Definition */
{
    cout<<"\nBjarne Stroustrup";
}
void main()
{
    printmyname();  /* Calling Function */
    printmyname();
    printmyname();
}
```

2. Program to understand the concepts of no return value and no argument function

```cpp
#include <iostream.h>
void printline()
{
    int i;
    cout<<"\n";
```

```
        for(i=1;i<=80;i++)
                cout<<"-";
}
void main()
{
        printline();
        cout<<"\t\t\tC++ Language is Developed by";
        printline();
        cout<<"\t\tBjarne Stroustrup";
        printline();
}
```

3. Program to understand the concepts of no return value with argument function

```
// Program 1
#include <iostream.h>
void printline(char c)
{
        int i;
        cout<<"\n";
        for(i=1;i<=80;i++)
                cout<<c;
}
void main()
{
        char ch='$';
        printline('a');
        cout<<"\t\t\tC++ Language is Developed by";
        printline(ch);
        cout<<"\t\tBjarne Stroustrup";
        printline('*');
}
```

```
// Program 2
#include <iostream.h>
void printline(char c, int n)
{
        int i;
        cout<<"\n";
        for(i=1;i<=n;i++)
                cout<<c;
}
void main()
{
        char ch='$';
        int n = 55;
        printline('a', 60);
        cout<<"\n\t\tC++ Language is Developed by";
        printline(ch, n);
        cout<<"\n\tBjarne Stroustrup";
        printline('*', 50);
}
```

4. Program to understand the concepts of return value without argument function

```cpp
// Program 1
#include <iostream.h>
int ret143()
{
     return 143;
}
void main()
{
     int n = 0;
     cout<<"\nBefore, calling function N = "<<n;
     n = ret143();
     cout<<"\nAfter, calling function N = "<<n;
}


// Program 2
#include <iostream.h>
float pi()
{
     return 3.14;
}
void main()
{
     float rad,area;
     cout<<"\nEnter Radius of the Circle : ";
     cin>>rad;
     area = pi() * rad * rad;
     cout<<"\nArea of the Circle is "<<area;
}
```

5. Program to understand the concepts of return value with argument function

```cpp
#include <iostream.h>
int cube(int a)
{
     return a*a*a;
}
int sqr(int x)
{
     return x*x;
}
void main()
{
     int n,res;
     cout<<"\nEnter number = ";
     cin>>n;
     res = sqr(n);
     cout<<"\nSquare of "<<n<<" = "<<res;
     res=cube(n);
     cout<<"\nCube of "<<n<<" = "<<res;
}
```

6. Program to find the factorial using function

```
#include <iostream.h>
long int fact(int n)
{
    int i;
    long int f=1;
    for(i=1;i<=n;i++)
        f=f*i;
    return f;
}
void main()
{
    int n;
    long f;
    cout<<"\nEnter number: ";
    cin>>n;
    f = fact(n);
    cout<<"\nFactorial of "<<n<<" is "<<f;
    f = fact(5);
    cout<<"\nFactorial of 5 is "<<f;
}
```

7. Program to calculate the average of three numbers using function

```
#include <iostream.h>
float avg3(int a,int b,int c)
{
    float r;
    r = (a+b+c)/3.0;      // return (a+b+c)/3.0;
    return r;
}
void main()
{
    int a,b,c;
    float d;
    cout<<"\nEnter three numbers\n";
    cin>>a>>b>>c;
    d = avg3(a,b,c);
    cout<<"\nAverage = "<<d;
}
```

8. Program to perform nCr calculation. nCr = n! / (r! * (n-r)!)

```
#include <iostream.h>
long int fact(int n)
{
    int i;
    long int f=1;
    for(i=1;i<=n;i++)
        f=f*i;
    return f;
}
```

```
void main()
{
    int n,r;
    long res;
    cout<<"\nEnter N Value : ";
    cin>>n;
    cout<<"\nEnter R Value : ";
    cin>>r;
    res = fact(n) /( fact(r) * fact(n-r) );
    cout<<"\nC("<<n<<","<<r<<") = "<<res;
}
```

9. Program to find the 'x' to the power 'n' using function

```
#include <iostream.h>
float power(float x,int n)
{
    float ans=1.0;
    int i;
    for(i=1;i<=n;i++)
        ans = ans * x;
    return ans;
}
void main()
{
    int n;
    float x,res;
    cout<<"Enter X Value :  ";
    cin>>x;
    cout<<"Enter N Value : ";
    cin>>n;
    res = power(x,n);
    cout<<"\n"<<x<<" to the power "<<n<<" is "<<res;
    res = power(x,2);
    cout<<"\n"<<x<<" to the power 2 is "<<res;
    res = power(2.0,n);
    cout<<"\n2.0 to the power "<<n<<" is "<<res;
}
```

10. Prerequisite program to understand the concepts of call by value

```
#include <iostream.h>
void main()
{
    int x = 5;
    int n = x;
    cout<<"\nX = "<<x;
    cout<<"\nN = "<<n;
    n++;
    cout<<"\nX = "<<x;
    cout<<"\nN = "<<n;
}
```

11. Program to understand the concepts of call by value

```
#include <iostream.h>
void change(int x)   // x is dummy or formal argument
{
     x = x + 10;
}
void main()
{
     int n;
     cout<<"\nGive N = ";
     cin>>n;
     cout<<"\nBefore Calling, N = "<<n;
     change(n); // n is original or actual argument
     cout<<"\nAfter Calling, N = "<<n;
}
```

12. Prerequisite program to understand the concepts of call by reference

```
#include <iostream.h>
void main()
{
     int x = 1;
     int &n = x;
     cout<<"\nX = "<<x;
     cout<<"\nN = "<<n;
     n = 10;
     cout<<"\nX = "<<x;
     cout<<"\nN = "<<n;
}
```

13. Program to understand the concepts of call by reference

```
#include <iostream.h>
void change(int &x) /* x is dummy or formal argument */
{
     x = x + 10;
}
void main()
{
     int n;
     cout<<"\nGive N = ";
     cin>>n;
     cout<<"\nBefore Calling, N = "<<n;
     change(n); /* n is original or actual argument */
     cout<<"\nAfter Calling, N = "<<n;
}
```

14. Program to calculate the sum and average of three numbers using function and call by reference

```
#include <iostream.h>
void sumavg3(int x,int y,int z,int &s,float &a)
{
    s = x + y + z;
    a = s / 3.0;
}
void main()
{
    int a,b,c,sum=0;
    float avg=0;
    cout<<"\nGive A, B and C values\n";
    cin>>a>>b>>c;
    cout<<"\nSum = "<<sum;
    cout<<"\nAverage = "<<avg;
    sumavg3(a,b,c,sum,avg);
    cout<<"\nSum = "<<sum;
    cout<<"\nAverage = "<<avg;
}
```

15. Program to understand the concepts of passing array as argument

```
#include <iostream.h>
void change(int x[],int n)
{
    int i;
    for(i=0;i<n;i++)
        x[i]+=10;
}
void main()
{
    int n[5]={10,20,30,40,50},i;
    cout<<"\nBefore calling, array contains\n";
    for(i=0;i<5;i++)
        cout<<"\n"<<n[i];
    change(n,5);
    cout<<"\nAfter calling, array contains\n";
    for(i=0;i<5;i++)
        cout<<"\n"<<n[i];
}
```

16. Program to understand the concepts of passing structure variable as argument

```
// Program 1
#include <iostream.h>
struct person
{
    char name[30];
    int age;
};
```

```
void printperson(struct person p)
{
    cout<<"\nName = "<<p.name;
    cout<<"\nAge = "<<p.age;
}
void main()
{
    struct person p1,p2;
    cout<<"\nEnter Person 1 Name and Age\n";
    cin>>p1.name>>p1.age;
    cout<<"\nEnter Person 2 Name and Age\n";
    cin>>p2.name>>p2.age;
    printperson(p1);
    printperson(p2);
}


// Program 2
#include <iostream.h>
struct person
{
    char name[30];
    int age;
};
void printperson(struct person p)
{
    cout<<"\nName = "<<p.name;
    cout<<"\nAge = "<<p.age;
}
void readperson(struct person &p)
{
    cout<<"\nEnter Person Name and Age\n";
    cin>>p.name>>p.age;
}
void main()
{
    struct person p1,p2;
    readperson(p1);
    readperson(p2);
    printperson(p1);
    printperson(p2);
}
```

17. Program to understand the concepts of function overloading

```
#include <iostream.h>
void printline()
{
    int i;
    cout<<"\n";
    for(i=1;i<=80;i++)
        cout<<"-";
}
```

```
void printline(char c)
{
    int i;
    cout<<"\n";
    for(i=1;i<=80;i++)
        cout<<c;
}
void printline(char c,int n)
{
    int i;
    cout<<"\n";
    for(i=1;i<=n;i++)
        cout<<c;
}
void main()
{
    char ch='#';
    int n=45;
    printline();
    printline('*');
    printline('$',70);
    printline(ch,n);
}
```

18. Program to understand the concepts of default argument function

```
#include <iostream.h>
void printline(char c='-',int n=80)
{
    int i;
    cout<<"\n";
    for(i=1;i<=n;i++)
        cout<<c;
}
void main()
{
    printline();
    printline('*');
    printline('^',50);
}
```

19. Program to find the 'x' to the power 'n' using default argument function

```
#include <iostream.h>
float power(float,int=3);
void main() {
    int a,b,c;
    float res;
    cout<<"\nEnter A, B and C Value\n";
    cin>>a>>b>>c;
    res = power(a)+power(b)+power(c);
    cout<<"\nResult = "<<res;
}
```

```
float power(float x,int n)
{
    float ans=1.0;
    int i;
    for(i=1;i<=n;i++)
        ans = ans * x;
    return ans;
}
```

20. Program to understand the concepts of inline function

```
#include <iostream.h>
inline float cube(float num)
{
    return num*num*num;
}
void main()
{
    float n;
    cout<<"\nEnter N Value : ";
    cin>>n;
    cout<<"\nCube of N is "<<cube(n);
}
```

3 CLASSES & OBJECTS PROGRAMS

1. Program to understand the concepts of classes and objects

```cpp
#include <iostream.h>
class circle
{
  private:
      float rad;
      float area;
      float circum;
  public:
      void read()
      {
          cout<<"\nEnter Radius : ";
          cin>>rad;
      }
      void calculate()
      {
          area = 3.14 * rad * rad;
          circum = 2 * 3.14 * rad;
      }
      void print()
      {
          cout<<"\nRadius = "<<rad;
          cout<<"\nArea = "<<area;
          cout<<"\nCircumference = "<<circum;
      }
};
void main()
{
      cout<<"\nMy first classes and objects in C++\n";
      circle c1;
      c1.print();
      c1.read();
      c1.print();
      c1.calculate();
      c1.print();
}
```

2. Program to understand the concepts of defining member function outside the class

```
#include<iostream.h>
class complex
{
  private:
      float real;
      float img;
  public:
      void read();
      void print();
      void conjugate();
};
void complex:: read()
{
      cout<<"\nEnter the complex (real img) number\n";
      cin>>real>>img;
}
void complex::print()
{
      cout<<"\nThe complex no. is "<<real;
      if(img>=0)
            cout<<"+";
      cout<<img<<"i\n";
}
void complex::conjugate()
{
      img = -img;
}
void main()
{
      complex c1;
      c1.print();
      c1.read();
      c1.print();
      c1.conjugate();
      c1.print();
}
```

3. Program to understand the concepts of making outside member function as an inline

```
#include<iostream.h>
class complex
{
  private:
      float real;
      float img;
  public:
      void read();
      void print();
};
```

```
inline void complex::read()
{
        cout<<"\nEnter the complex (real img) number\n";
        cin>>real>>img;
}
void complex::print()
{
        cout<<"\nThe complex no. is "<<real;
        if(img>=0)
                cout<<"+";
        cout<<img<<"i";
}
void main()
{
        complex c1;
        c1.read();
        c1.print();
}
```

4. Program to understand the concepts of nesting of member function

```
#include <iostream.h>
class circle
{
  private:
        float rad;
        float area;
  public:
        void read()
        {
                cout<<"\nEnter Radius = ";
                cin>>rad;
                calculate();
        }
        void calculate()
        {
                area = 3.14 * rad * rad;
        }
        void print()
        {
                cout<<"\nRadius = "<<rad;
                cout<<"\nArea   = "<<area;
        }
};
void main()
{
        circle c1;
        c1.read();
        c1.print();
}
```

5. Program to understand the concepts of private member function

```cpp
#include <iostream.h>
class circle
{
 private:
     float rad;
     float area;
     void calculate()
     {
         area = 3.14 * rad * rad;
     }
 public:
     void read()
     {
         cout<<"\nEnter Radius = ";
         cin>>rad;
     }
     void print()
     {
         calculate();
         cout<<"\nRadius = "<<rad;
         cout<<"\nArea   = "<<area;
     }
};
void main()
{
     circle c1;
     c1.read();
     c1.print();
}
```

6. Program to understand the concepts of array within a class

```cpp
// Program 1
#include <iostream.h>
class person
{
 private:
     char name[30];
     int age;
 public:
     void read()
     {
         cout<<"\nEnter Name and Age\n";
         cin>>name>>age;
     }
     void print()
     {
         cout<<"\nName = "<<name;
         cout<<"\nAge  = "<<age;
     }
};
```

```
void main()
{
    person p1;
    p1.read();
    p1.print();
}

// Program 2
#include <iostream.h>
class stud
{
  private:
    long regno;
    char name[30];
    int mark[3];
    int tot;
    float per;
  public:
    void read()
    {
        int i;
        cout<<"\nEnter register number: ";
        cin>>regno;
        cout<<"\nEnter name: ";
        cin>>name;
        cout<<"\nEnter 3 subject marks one by one\n";
        tot = 0;
        for(i=0;i<3;i++)
        {
            cin>>mark[i];
            tot += mark[i];
        }
        per = tot / 3.0;
    }
    void print()
    {
        int i;
        cout<<"\nRegister number: "<<regno;
        cout<<"\nName: "<<name;
        for(i=0;i<3;i++)
            cout<<"\nSubject "<<i+1<<" Mark: "<<mark[i];
        cout<<"\nTotal: "<<tot;
        cout<<"\nPercentage: "<<per;
    }
};
void main()
{
    stud s1;
    s1.read();
    s1.print();
}
```

7. Program to understand the concepts of array of objects

```cpp
#include <iostream.h>
class person
{
  private:
      char name[30];
      int age;
  public:
      void read()
      {
          cout<<"\nEnter Name and Age\n";
          cin>>name>>age;
      }
      void print()
      {
          cout<<"\nName = "<<name;
          cout<<"\nAge  = "<<age;
      }
};
void main()
{
      person p[25];
      int n,i;
      cout<<"\nEnter Number of Persons: ";
      cin>>n;
      cout<<"\nEnter "<<n<<" Person Details one by one\n";
      for(i=0;i<n;i++)
          p[i].read();
      cout<<"\nPersons details\n";
      for(i=0;i<n;i++)
          p[i].print();
}
```

8. Program to understand the concepts of passing arguments to member function

```cpp
#include <iostream.h>
class complex
{
  private:
      float real;
      float img;
  public:
      void read()
      {
          cout<<"\nEnter Complex Number (Real, Img)\n";
          cin>>real>>img;
      }
      void print() {
          cout<<"\nThe Complex Number is "<<real;
          if(img>=0)
              cout<<"+";
          cout<<img<<"i";
      }
```

```
        void putdata(float r,float i)
        {
              real = r;
              img = i;
        }
};
void main()
{
        complex c1,c2;
        c1.read();
        c2.putdata(143,786);
        c1.print();
        c2.print();
}
```

9. Program to understand the concepts of member function overloading

```
#include <iostream.h>
class complex
{
  private:
        float real;
        float img;
  public:
        void read()
        {
              cout<<"\nEnter Complex Number (Real, Img)\n";
              cin>>real>>img;
        }
        void print()
        {
              cout<<"\nThe Complex Number is "<<real;
              if(img>=0)
                    cout<<"+";
              cout<<img<<"i";
        }
        void putdata(float r,float i)
        {
              real = r;
              img = i;
        }
        void putdata(float v)
        {
              real = img = v; // putdata(v,v);
        }
        void putdata()
        {
              real = img = 0; // pudata(0);
        }
};
```

```
void main()
{
    complex c1,c2,c3;
    c1.putdata(1.2,3.4);
    c2.putdata(5.6);
    c3.putdata();
    c1.print();
    c2.print();
    c3.print();
}
```

10. Program to understand the concepts of default argument member function

```
#include <iostream.h>
class complex
{
  private:
    float real;
    float img;
  public:
    void read()
    {
        cout<<"\nEnter Complex Number (Real, Img)\n";
        cin>>real>>img;
    }
    void print()
    {
        cout<<"\nThe Complex Number is "<<real;
        if(img>=0)
            cout<<"+";
        cout<<img<<"i";
    }
    void putdata(float r = 0,float i = 0)
    {
        real = r;
        img = i;
    }
};
void main()
{
    complex c1,c2,c3;
    c1.putdata(1.2,3.4);
    c2.putdata(5.6);
    c3.putdata();
    c1.print();
    c2.print();
    c3.print();
}
```

11. Program to understand the concepts of returning a value (member function)

```cpp
#include<iostream.h>
class complex
{
  private:
      float real;
      float img;
  public:
      void read()
      {
          cout<<"\nEnter Complex Number (Real, Img)\n";
          cin>>real>>img;
      }
      void print()
      {
          cout<<"\nThe Complex Number is "<<real;
          if(img>=0)
              cout<<"+";
          cout<<img<<"i";
      }
      float getreal()
      {
          return real;
      }
      float getimg()
      {
          return img;
      }
};
void main()
{
      complex c1,c2;
      c1.read();
      c2 = c1;
      c1.print();
      cout<<"\nReal Part = "<<c1.getreal();
      cout<<"\nImaginary Part  = "<<c2.getimg();
      c2.print();
}
```

12. Program to understand the concepts of passing object as argument

```cpp
#include <iostream.h>
class complex
{
  private:
      float real;
      float img;
  public:
      void read() {
          cout<<"\nEnter Complex Number (Real, Img)\n";
          cin>>real>>img;
      }
```

```cpp
        void print()
        {
            cout<<"\nThe Complex Number is "<<real;
            if(img>=0)
                cout<<"+";
            cout<<img<<"i";
        }
        void putdata(float r,float i)
        {
            real = r;
            img = i;
        }
        void add(complex c)
        {
            real = real + c.real;
            img = img + c.img;
        }
};
void main()
{
    complex c1,c2;
    c1.putdata(1.2,3.4);
    c2.putdata(5.6,7.8);
    c1.print();
    c2.print();
    c1.add(c2); // c1=c1+c2;
    c1.print();
    c2.print();
}
```

13. Program to understand the concepts of returning an object

```cpp
#include<iostream.h>
class complex
{
  private:
        float real;
        float img;
  public:
        void read()
        {
            cout<<"\nEnter Complex Number (Real, Img)\n";
            cin>>real>>img;
        }
        void print()
        {
            cout<<"\nThe Complex Number is "<<real;
            if(img>=0)
                cout<<"+";
            cout<<img<<"i";
        }
```

```
        void putdata(float r = 0,float i = 0)
        {
            real = r;
            img = i;
        }
        complex add(complex c)
        {
            complex t;
            t.real = real + c.real;
            t.img  = img + c.img;
            return t;
            /* c.real = real + c.real;
            c.img = img + c.img;
            return c; */
        }
};
void main()
{
    complex c1,c2,c3;
    c1.putdata(1.2,3.4);
    c2.putdata(5.6,7.8);
    c1.print();
    c2.print();
    c3.print();
    c3=c1.add(c2); // c3=c1+c2;
    c1.print();
    c2.print();
    c3.print();
}
```

14. Program to understand the concepts of friend function

```
// Program 1
#include <iostream.h>
class complex
{
  private:
        float real;
        float img;
  public:
     void read()
     {
        cout<<"\nEnter Complex Number (Real, Img)\n";
        cin>>real>>img;
     }
     friend void printcomplex(complex);
};
void printcomplex(complex c)
{
    cout<<"\nThe Complex Number is "<<c.real;
    if(c.img>=0)
        cout<<"+";
    cout<<c.img<<"i";
}
```

```cpp
void main()
{
    complex c1;
    c1.read();
    printcomplex(c1);
}

// Program 2
#include <iostream.h>
class complex
{
  private:
      float real;
      float img;
  public:
      void read()
      {
          cout<<"\nEnter Complex Number (Real, Img)\n";
          cin>>real>>img;
      }
      void print()
      {
          cout<<"\nThe Complex Number is "<<real;
          if(img>=0)
              cout<<"+";
          cout<<img<<"i";
      }
      void putdata(float r = 0,float i = 0)
      {
          real = r;
          img = i;
      }
          friend complex add(complex,complex);
};
complex add(complex c1,complex c2)
{
    complex t;
    t.real = c1.real + c2.real;
    t.img = c1.img + c2.img;
    return t;
}
void main()
{
    complex c1,c2,c3;
    c1.putdata(1.2,3.4);
    c2.putdata(5.6,7.8);
    c1.print();
    c2.print();
    c3.print();
    c3=add(c1,c2); // c3=c1+c2;
    c1.print();
    c2.print();
    c3.print();
}
```

15. Program to understand the concepts of static member variable or class variable

```cpp
// Program 1
#include <iostream.h>
class circle
{
  private:
      float rad;
      static float area;
  public:
      void read()
      {
          cout<<"\nEnter Radius: ";
          cin>>rad;
      }
      void calculate()
      {
          area = 3.14 * rad * rad;
      }
      void print()
      {
          cout<<"\nRadius: "<<rad;
          cout<<"\nArea: "<<area;
      }
};
float circle::area;
void main()
{
      circle c1,c2;
      c1.read();
      c2.read();
      c1.calculate();
      c1.print();
      c2.print();
      c2.calculate();
      c2.print();
      c1.print();
}

// Program 2
#include <iostream.h>
class Book
{
  private:
      int isbn;
      char name[30];
      char author[30];
  public:
      static int tot_book;
      void read()
      {
          cout<<"\nEnter ISBN, Book & Author Name one by one\n";
          cin>>isbn>>name>>author;
          tot_book++;
      }
```

```cpp
        void print()
        {
            cout<<"\nISBN   = "<<isbn;
            cout<<"\nName   = "<<name;
            cout<<"\nAuthor = "<<author;
        }
};
int Book::tot_book=100;
void main()
{
    Book b1,b2;
    cout<<"\nTotal Number of Books: "<<Book::tot_book;
    b1.read();
    b2.read();
    b1.print();
    b2.print();
    cout<<"\nTotal Number of Books: "<<Book::tot_book;
}
```

16. Program to understand the concepts of static member function or class function

```cpp
// Program 1
#include <iostream.h>
class circle
{
  private:
    float rad;
    static float area;
  public:
    void read()
    {
        cout<<"\nEnter Radius: ";
        cin>>rad;
    }
    void calculate()
    {
        area = 3.14 * rad * rad;
    }
    void print()
    {
        cout<<"\nRadius: "<<rad;
        cout<<"\nArea: "<<area;
    }
    static void showarea()
    {
        cout<<"\nArea: "<<area;
    }
};
float circle::area;
void main()
{
    circle::showarea();
    circle c1,c2;
    c1.read();
    c2.read();
```

```cpp
        c1.calculate();
        c1.print();
        c2.calculate();
        c2.print();
}

// Program 2
#include <iostream.h>
class Book
{
  private:
        int isbn;
        char name[30];
        char author[30];
        static int tot_book;
  public:
        void read()
        {
            cout<<"\nEnter ISBN, Book & Author Name one by one\n";
            cin>>isbn>>name>>author;
            tot_book++;
        }
        void print()
        {
            cout<<"\nISBN   = "<<isbn;
            cout<<"\nName   = "<<name;
            cout<<"\nAuthor = "<<author;
        }
          static void available_book()
          {
            cout<<"\nTotal Book = "<<tot_book;
          }
};
int Book::tot_book;
void main()
{
        Book::available_book();
        Book b1,b2;
        b1.available_book();
        b1.read();
        b1.available_book();
        b2.read();
        b2.available_book();
        b1.print();
        b2.print();
        Book::available_book();
}
```

4 CONSTRUCTORS & DESTRUCTORS PROGRAMS

1. Program to understand the concepts of constructor

```cpp
// Program 1
#include <iostream.h>
class distance
{
  private:
      float feet;
      float inches;
  public:
      distance() // default constructor
      {
          feet=0;
          inches=0;
      }
      void read()
      {
          cout<<"\nEnter Distance (Feet Inches)\n";
          cin>>feet>>inches;
      }
      void print()
      {
          cout<<"\nThe Distance is "<<feet<<"' "<<inches<<"\"\n";
      }
};
void main()
{
      distance d1;
      d1.print();
      d1.read();
      d1.print();
}
```

```cpp
// Program 2
#include <iostream.h>
class date
{
  private:
      int dd;
      int mm;
      int yyyy;
  public:
      date()
      {
          dd = 30;
          mm = 12;
          yyyy = 1950;
      }
      void read()
      {
          cout<<"\nEnter Date (dd mm yyyy)\n";
          cin>>dd>>mm>>yyyy;
      }
      void print()
      {
          cout<<"\nThe Date is "<<dd<<"-"<<mm<<"-"<<yyyy;
      }
};
void main()
{
      date d1;
      d1.print();
      d1.read();
      d1.print();
}
```

2. Program to understand the concepts of destructor

```cpp
#include <iostream.h>
class distance
{
  private:
      int feet;
      float inches;
  public:
      distance()
      {
          feet=0;
          inches=0;
      }
      ~distance()
      {
          cout<<"\nObject is Deleted\n";
      }
      void read()
      {
          cout<<"\nEnter Distance (Feet Inches)\n";
```

```
            cin>>feet>>inches;
        }
        void print()
        {
            cout<<"\nThe Distance is "<<feet<<"' "<<inches<<"\"\n";
        }
};
void fun()
{
    distance d1,d2;
}
void main()
{
    distance d1,d2;
    d1.print();
    d2.print();
    fun();
    d1.print();
    d2.print();
    fun();
}
```

3. Program to understand the concepts of constructor overloading

```
// Program 1
#include <iostream.h>
class date
{
  private:
        int dd;
        int mm;
        int yyyy;
  public:
        date()
        {
            dd = 0;
            mm = 0;
            yyyy = 0;
        }
        date(int d,int m,int y)
        {
            dd = d;
            mm = m;
            yyyy = y;
        }
        void read()
        {
            cout<<"\nEnter Date (dd mm yyyy)\n";
            cin>>dd>>mm>>yyyy;
        }
        void print() {
            cout<<"\nThe Date is "<<dd<<"-"<<mm<<"-"<<yyyy;
        }
};
```

```
void main()
{
    date d1,d2(30,12,1950),d3(15,8,1872),d4(21,2,1978);
    d1.print();
    d2.print();
    d3.print();
    d4.print();
}

// Program 2
#include <iostream.h>
class complex
{
 private:
    float real;
    float img;
 public:
    complex()
    {
        real = 0;
        img = 0;
    }
    complex(float r,float i)
    {
        real = r;
        img = i;
    }
    complex(float v)
    {
        real = img = v;
    }
    void read()
    {
        cout<<"\nEnter Complex Number (Real, Img)\n";
        cin>>real>>img;
    }
    void print()
    {
        cout<<"\nThe Complex Number is "<<real;
        if(img>=0)
            cout<<"+";
        cout<<img<<"i";
    }
};
void main()
{
    complex c1,c2(1.2,3.4),c3(5.6),c4=7.8;
    c1.print();
    c2.print();
    c3.print();
    c4.print();
}
```

4. Program to understand the concepts of default argument constructor

```cpp
#include <iostream.h>
class complex
{
 private:
     float real;
     float img;
 public:
     complex(float r = 0,float i = 0)
     {
         real = r;
         img = i;
     }
     void read()
     {
         cout<<"\nEnter Complex Number (Real, Img)\n";
         cin>>real>>img;
     }
     void print()
     {
         cout<<"\nThe Complex Number is "<<real;
         if(img>=0)
             cout<<"+";
         cout<<img<<"i";
     }
};
void main()
{
     complex c1,c2(1.2,3.4),c3(5.6),c4=7.8;
     c1.print();
     c2.print();
     c3.print();
     c4.print();
}
```

5. Program to understand the concepts of dynamic initialization of constructor

```cpp
#include <iostream.h>
class complex
{
 private:
     float real;
     float img;
 public:
     complex()
     {
         real = 0;
         img = 0;
     }
     complex(float r,float i) {
         real = r;
         img = i;
     }
```

```
        void read()
        {
                cout<<"\nEnter Complex Number (Real, Img)\n";
                cin>>real>>img;
        }
        void print()
        {
                cout<<"\nThe Complex Number is "<<real;
                if(img>=0)
                        cout<<"+";
                cout<<img<<"i";
        }
};
void main()
{
        complex c1;
        float r,i;
        cout<<"\nEnter Real and Imaginary Value\n";
        cin>>r>>i;
        complex c2(r,i); //implicit
        complex c3 = complex(r,i); //explicit
        complex c4;
        c4 = complex(r,i);
        c1.print();
        c2.print();
        c3.print();
        c4.print();
}
```

6. Program to understand the concepts of copy constructor

```
#include <iostream.h>
class complex
{
  private:
        float real;
        float img;
  public:
        complex()
        {
                real = 0;
                img = 0;
        }
        complex(float r,float i)
        {
                real = r;
                img = i;
        }
        complex(complex &d)
        {
                real = d.real;
                img = d.img;
        }
```

```
    void read()
    {
        cout<<"\nEnter Complex Number (Real, Img)\n";
        cin>>real>>img;
    }
    void print()
    {
        cout<<"\nThe Complex Number is "<<real;
        if(img>=0)
            cout<<"+";
        cout<<img<<"i";
    }
};
void main()
{
    complex c1(1.2,3.4),c2=c1;
    c1.print();
    c2.print();
}
```

7. Program to understand the concepts of dynamic memory allocation and garbage collection using new and delete operator

```
// Program 1
#include<iostream.h>
void main()
{
    int *ip;
    ip = new int(123);
    cout<<"\nIP = "<<*ip;
    *ip = 5;
    cout<<"\nIP = "<<*ip;
    delete ip;
}
```

```
// Program 2
#include<iostream.h>
void main()
{
    int *ip,n,i;
    cout<<"\nEnter number of elements: ";
    cin>>n;
    ip = new int[n];
    cout<<"\nEnter "<<n<<" numbers one by one\n";
    for(i=0;i<n;i++)
        cin>>*(ip+i);
    cout<<"\nGiven numbers\n";
    for(i=0;i<n;i++)
        cout<<*(ip+i)<<"\n";
    delete []ip;
}
```

8. Program to understand the concepts of dynamic constructor

```
#include<iostream.h>
#include <string.h>
class string
{
  private:
      char *str;
      int n;
  public:
      string()
      {
          str='\0';
          n=0;
      }
      string(char s[])
      {
          n = strlen(s);
          str = new char[n+1];
          strcpy(str,s);
      }
      void print()
      {
          cout<<"\nString is "<<str;
      }
};
void main()
{
      string s1,s2("Bjarne"),s3("Stroustrup");
      s1.print();
      s2.print();
      s3.print();
}
```

9. Program to understand the concepts of dynamic constructor & destructor

```
#include<iostream.h>
#include <string.h>
class string
{
  private:
      char *str;
      int n;
  public:
      string()
      {
          str='\0';
          n=0;
      }
```

```
        ~string()
        {
            delete []str;
        }
        string(char s[])
        {
            n = strlen(s);
            str = new char[n+1];
            strcpy(str,s);
        }
        void print()
        {
            cout<<"\nString is "<<str;
        }
};
void main()
{
    string s1,s2("Bjarne"),s3("Stroustrup");
    s1.print();
    s2.print();
    s3.print();
}
```

5 OPERATOR OVERLOADING PROGRAMS

1. Prerequisite program to understand the concepts of operator overloading

```
#include <iostream.h>
void main()
{
    int i=10,j=20,k;
    float a=1.2,b=3.5,c;
    k = i + j;
    cout<<"\nK = "<<k;
    c = a + b;
    cout<<"\nC = "<<c;
    c = i + b;
    cout<<"\nC = "<<c;
    k = a + k;
    cout<<"\nK = "<<k;
    k = -i;
    cout<<"\nK = "<<k;
    cout<<"\nI = "<<i;
}
```

2. Program to understand the concepts of unary operator overloading

```
// Program 1
#include <iostream.h>
class complex
{
 private:
    float real;
    float img;
 public:
    complex()
    {
        real = 0;
        img = 0;
    }
```

```cpp
        void read()
        {
            cout<<"\nEnter Complex Number (Real, Img)\n";
            cin>>real>>img;
        }
        void print()
        {
            cout<<"\nThe Complex Number is "<<real;
            if(img>=0)
                cout<<"+";
            cout<<img<<"i";
        }
        complex operator -()
        {
            complex t;
            t.real = -real;
            t.img = -img;
            return t;
        }
};
void main()
{
    complex c1,c2;
    c1.read();
    c2 = -c1;
    c1.print();
    c2.print();
}

// Program 2
#include <iostream.h>
class distance
{
  private:
    int feet;
    float inches;
  public:
    void read()
    {
        cout<<"\nEnter Distance (Feet Inches)\n";
        cin>>feet>>inches;
    }
    void print()
    {
        cout<<"\nThe Distance is "<<feet<<"' "<<inches<<"\"\n";
    }
    distance operator ++()
    {
        feet++;
        inches++;
        return *this;
    }
```

```
        distance operator ++(int)
        {
            feet++;
            inches++;
            return *this;
        }
        distance operator -()
        {
            distance d;
            d.feet = -feet;
            d.inches = -inches;
            return d;
        }
};
void main()
{
        distance d1,d2;
        d1.read();
        d1.print();
        d2=++d1;
        d1.print();
        d2.print();
        d2.read();
        d2.print();
        d1=-d2;
        d1.print();
        d2.print();
        d1=d2++;
        d1.print();
        d2.print();
}
```

3. Program to understand the concepts of binary operator overloading

```
#include <iostream.h>
#include <math.h>
class complex
{
  private:
        float real;
        float img;
  public:
        complex(float r=0,float i=0)
        {
            real = r;
            img = i;
        }
        void read()
        {
            cout<<"\nEnter Complex Number (Real, Img)\n";
            cin>>real>>img;
        }
```

```cpp
        void print()
        {
            cout<<"\nThe Complex Number is "<<real;
            if(img>=0)
                cout<<"+";
            cout<<img<<"i";
        }
        complex operator + (complex c)
        {
            /* complex t;
            t.real = real + c.real;
            t.img = img + c.img;
            return t;*/
            /*c.real = real + c.real;
            c.img = img + c.img;
            return c;*/
            return complex(real+c.real,img+c.img);
        }
        complex operator * (complex c)
        {
            float mag1 = sqrt(real*real+img*img);
            float mag2 = sqrt(c.real*c.real+c.img*c.img);
            float ang1 = atan(img/real);
            float ang2 = atan(c.img/c.real);
            mag1 *= mag2;
            ang1 += ang2;
            c.real = mag1 * cos(ang1);
            c.img = mag1 * sin(ang1);
            return c;
        }
};
void main()
{
    complex c1,c2,c3;
    c1.read();
    c2.read();
    c3=c1+c2;
    c1.print();
    c2.print();
    c3.print();
    c3=c1*c2;
    c3.print();
}
```

4. Program to understand the concepts of relational operator overloading

```cpp
#include <iostream.h>
class complex
{
 private:
    float real;
    float img;
```

```
public:
    void read()
    {
        cout<<"\nEnter Complex Number (Real, Img)\n";
        cin>>real>>img;
    }
    void print()
    {
        cout<<"\nThe Complex Number is "<<real;
        if(img>=0)
            cout<<"+";
        cout<<img<<"i";
    }
    int operator == (complex c)
    {
        if(real == c.real && img == c.img)
            return 1;
        else
            return 0;
    }
};
void main()
{
    complex c1,c2;
    c1.read();
    c2.read();
    c1.print();
    c2.print();
    if(c1 == c2)
        cout<<"\nC1 object is equal to C2";
    else
        cout<<"\nC1 object is not equal to C2";
}
```

5. Program to understand the concepts of unary operator overloading using friend function

```
#include <iostream.h>
class distance
{
  private:
      int feet;
      float inches;
  public:
      distance(int f=0,float i=0.0)
      {
          feet = f;
          inches = i;
      }
      void read()
      {
          cout<<"\nEnter Distance (Feet Inches)\n";
          cin>>feet>>inches;
      }
```

```cpp
        void print()
        {
                cout<<"\nThe Distance is "<<feet<<"' "<<inches<<"\"\n";
        }
        friend distance operator ++(distance&);
        friend distance operator -(distance);
};
distance operator ++(distance &d)
{
        d.feet++;
        d.inches++;
        return d;
}
distance operator -(distance d)
{
        return distance(-d.feet,-d.inches);
}
void main()
{
        distance d1,d2;
        d1.read();
        d2 = ++d1;
        d1.print();
        d2.print();
        d1 = -d2;
        d1.print();
        d2.print();
}
```

6. Program to understand the concepts of binary operator overloading using friend function

```cpp
#include <iostream.h>
class complex
{
  private:
        float real;
        float img;
  public:
        void read()
        {
                cout<<"\nEnter Complex Number (Real, Img)\n";
                cin>>real>>img;
        }
        void print()
        {
                cout<<"\nThe Complex Number is "<<real;
                if(img>=0)
                        cout<<"+";
                cout<<img<<"i";
        }
        friend complex operator + (complex,complex);
};
```

```
complex operator + (complex c1,complex c2) {
    complex t;
    t.real = c1.real + c2.real;
    t.img = c1.img + c2.img;
    return t;
}
void main() {
    complex c1,c2,c3;
    c1.read();
    c2.read();
    c3=c1+c2;
    c1.print();
    c2.print();
    c3.print();
}
```

7. Program to understand the concepts of relational operator overloading using friend function

```
#include <iostream.h>
class complex {
  private:
    float real;
    float img;
  public:
    void read() {
        cout<<"\nEnter Complex Number (Real, Img)\n";
        cin>>real>>img;
    }
    void print() {
        cout<<"\nThe Complex Number is "<<real;
        if(img>=0)
            cout<<"+";
        cout<<img<<"i";
    }
    friend int operator < (complex,complex);
};
int operator < (complex c1,complex c2) {
    if(c1.real<c2.real || c1.img<c2.img)
        return 1;
    else
        return 0;
}
void main() {
    complex c1,c2;
    c1.read();
    c2.read();
    c1.print();
    c2.print();
    if(c1<c2)
        cout<<"\nC1 object is smaller than C2";
    else
        cout<<"\nC2 object is smaller than C1";
}
```

6 TYPE CONVERSION PROGRAMS

1. Program to understand the concepts of basic to basic conversion

```cpp
#include <iostream.h>
void main()
{
    int a=10;
    float b;
    b = a;
    cout<<"\nA = "<<a;
    cout<<"\nB = "<<b;
    b = 123.456;
    a = int(b);
    cout<<"\nA = "<<a;
    cout<<"\nB = "<<b;
}
```

2. Program to understand the concepts of basic to class conversion

```cpp
// Program 1
#include <iostream.h>
#include <math.h>
class distance
{
  private:
    int feet;
    float inches;
  public:
    distance()
    {
        feet = inches = 0;
    }
    distance(int f,float i)
    {
        feet=f;
        inches=i;
    }
```

```
        distance(float  i)
        {
            feet=i/12;
            inches=fmod(i,12);
        }
        void read()
        {
            cout<<"\nEnter Distance (Feet Inches)\n";
            cin>>feet>>inches;
        }
        void print()
        {
            cout<<"\nThe Distance is "<<feet<<"' "<<inches<<"\"\n";
        }
};
void main()
{
    float in;
    distance d1;
    cout<<"\nEnter Distance in Inches : ";
    cin>>in;
    d1 = in;
    d1.print();
}

// Program 2
#include <iostream.h>
class time
{
  private:
        int hh;
        int mm;
        int ss;
  public:
        time()
        {
            hh=mm=ss=0;
        }
        time(int ts)
        {
            hh = ts / 3600;
            ts = ts % 3600;
            mm = ts / 60;
            ss = ts % 60;
        }
        time(int h,int m,int s)
        {
            hh = h;
            mm = m;
            ss = s;
        }
```

```cpp
        void read()
        {
            cout<<"\nEnter Time (hh mm ss)\n";
            cin>>hh>>mm>>ss;
        }
        void print()
        {
            cout<<"\nTime is "<<hh<<":"<<mm<<":"<<ss;
        }
};
void main()
{
    time t1,t2=3661,t3(3661);
    int s;
    cout<<"\nEnter Time in Seconds : ";
    cin>>s;
    t1 = time(s);
    t1.print();
    t2.print();
    t3.print();
}
```

3. Program to understand the concepts of class to basic conversion

```cpp
// Program 1
#include <iostream.h>
class time
{
  private:
        int hh;
        int mm;
        int ss;
  public:
        void read()
        {
            cout<<"\nEnter Time (hh mm ss)\n";
            cin>>hh>>mm>>ss;
        }
        void print()
        {
            cout<<"\nTime is "<<hh<<":"<<mm<<":"<<ss;
        }
        operator int()
        {
            return hh*3600+mm*60+ss;
        }
};
void main() {
    time t1;
    int s;
    t1.read();
    s = t1; // s = int(t1);
    cout<<"\nTime in Seconds = "<<s;
}
```

```
// Program 2
#include <iostream.h>
#include <math.h>
class distance
{
  private:
      int feet;
      float inches;
  public:
      distance()
      {
          feet = inches = 0;
      }
      distance(int f,float i)
      {
          feet=f;
          inches=i;
      }
      void read()
      {
          cout<<"\nEnter Distance (Feet Inches)\n";
          cin>>feet>>inches;
      }
      void print()
      {
          cout<<"\nThe Distance is "<<feet<<"' "<<inches<<"\"\n";
      }
      operator float()
      {
          float i;
          i = feet * 12 + inches;
          return i;
      }
};
void main()
{
      float in;
      distance d1;
      d1.read();
      in = d1; // in = float(d1);
      d1.print();
      cout<<"\nTotal Inches : "<<in<<"\"";
}
```

4. Program to understand the concepts of class to class conversion

```
#include <iostream.h>
class dm
{
  private:
      float m;
```

```cpp
    public:
        dm() {
            m = 0;
        }
        dm(float v) {
            m = v;
        }
        void read() {
            cout<<"\nEnter distance in metre : ";
            cin>>m;
        }
        void print() {
            cout<<"\nDistance in metres is "<<m<<"m\n";
        }
        float getm() {
            return m;
        }
};
class dcm
{
  private:
        float cm;
  public:
        dcm() {
            cm = 0;
        }
        dcm(dm obj) {
            cm = obj.getm() * 100;
        }
        void read() {
            cout<<"\nEnter distance in centi metre : ";
            cin>>cm;
        }
        void print() {
            cout<<"\nDistance in centi metres is "<<cm<<"cm\n";
        }
        operator dm() {
            dm t=cm/100;
            return t;
        }
};
void main()
{
    dm m1;
    dcm cm1;
    m1.read();
    cm1 = m1; // cm1 = dcm(m1);
    cm1.print();
    cm1.read();
    m1 = cm1;  // m1 = dm(cm1);
    m1.print();
}
```

7 INHERITANCE PROGRAMS

1. Program to understand the concepts of single inheritance

```cpp
#include <iostream.h>
class stud
{
  protected:
      int regno;
      char name[30];
  public:
      void getstud()
      {
          cout<<"\nEnter Register Number: ";
          cin>>regno;
          cout<<"\nEnter Name: ";
          cin>>name;
      }
      void showstud()
      {
          cout<<"\nRegister Number: "<<regno;
          cout<<"\nName: "<<name;
      }
};
class personal_info : public stud
{
  private:
      char addr[70];
      char place[30];
  public:
      void read()
      {
          getstud();
          cout<<"\nEnter Address: "; cin>>addr;
          cout<<"\nEnter Place: "; cin>>place;
      }
```

```cpp
        void print()
        {
            showstud();
            cout<<"\nAddress: "<<addr;
            cout<<"\nPlace: "<<place;
        }
};
void main()
{
    personal_info p1;
    p1.read();
    p1.print();
    p1.showstud();
}
```

2. Program to understand the concepts of overriding member function

```cpp
#include <iostream.h>
class stud
{
  protected:
    int regno;
    char name[30];
  public:
    void read()
    {
        cout<<"\nEnter Register Number: ";
        cin>>regno;
        cout<<"\nEnter Name: ";
        cin>>name;
    }
    void print()
    {
        cout<<"\nRegister Number: "<<regno;
        cout<<"\nName: "<<name;
    }
};
class personal_info : public stud
{
  private:
    char addr[70];
    char place[30];
  public:
    void read()
    {
        stud::read();
        cout<<"\nEnter Address: "; cin>>addr;
        cout<<"\nEnter Place: "; cin>>place;
    }
```

```
        void print()
        {
            stud::print();
            cout<<"\nAddress: "<<addr;
            cout<<"\nPlace: "<<place;
        }
};
void main()
{
    personal_info p1;
    p1.read();
    p1.print();
}
```


3. Program to understand the concepts of multiple inheritance

```
#include <iostream.h>
class circle
{
  protected:
    float rad;
  public:
    void getrad()
    {
        cout<<"\nEnter Radius: ";
        cin>>rad;
    }
    void showrad()
    {
        cout<<"\nRadius = "<<rad;
    }
};
class rect
{
  protected:
    float l;
    float b;
  public:
    void getlb()
    {
        cout<<"\nEnter the length: ";
        cin>>l;
        cout<<"\nEnter the breadth:";
        cin>>b;
    }
    void showlb()
    {
        cout<<"\nLength = "<<l;
        cout<<"\nBreadth = "<<b;
    }
};
```

```cpp
class Area : public circle, public rect
{
  private:
      float carea;
      float rarea;
  public:
      void read()
      {
          getrad();
          getlb();
      }
      void calculate()
      {
          carea = 3.14 * rad * rad;
          rarea = l * b;
      }
      void print()
      {
          showrad();
          cout<<"\nCircle Area = "<<carea;
          showlb();
          cout<<"\nRectangle Area = "<<rarea;
      }
};
void main()
{
      Area a1;
      a1.read();
      a1.calculate();
      a1.print();
}
```

4. Program to understand the concepts of multi-level inheritance

```cpp
#include <iostream.h>
class A
{
  protected:
      int a;
  public:
      void getA()
      {
          cout<<"\nEnter A: "; cin>>a;
      }
      void putA(int a)
      {
          this->a = a;
      }
      void showA()
      {
          cout<<"\nA = "<<this->a;
      }
};
```

```
class AB : public A
{
  protected:
      int b;
  public:
      void getAB()
      {
          getA();
          cout<<"\nEnter B: "; cin>>b;
      }
      void putAB(int a,int b)
      {
          this->a = a;      // putA(a);
          this->b = b;
      }
      void showAB()
      {
          showA();
          cout<<"\nB = "<<b;
      }
};
class ABC : public AB
{
  protected:
      int c;
  public:
      void read()
      {
          getAB();
          cout<<"\nEnter C: "; cin>>c;
      }
      void putdata(int a,int b,int c)
      {
          putAB(a,b);
          this->c = c;
      }
      void print()
      {
          showAB();
          cout<<"\nC = "<<c;
      }
};
void main()
{
      ABC a1;
      a1.read();
      a1.print();
      a1.putdata(123,456,789);
      a1.print();
}
```

5. Program to understand the concepts of hybrid inheritance

```cpp
#include <iostream.h>
class A
{
  protected:
      int a;
  public:
      void read()
      {
            cout<<"Enter A : ";
            cin>>a;
      }
      void putdata(int a)
      {
            this->a = a;
      }
      void print()
      {
            cout<<"\nA = "<<a;
      }
};
class AB : public A
{
  protected:
      int b;
  public:
      void read()
      {
            A::read();
            cout<<"Enter B : ";
            cin>>b;
      }
      void putdata(int a,int b)
      {
            A::putdata(a);
            this->b = b;
      }
      void print()
      {
            A::print();
            cout<<"\nB = "<<b;
      }
};
class res
{
  protected:
      int ans;
  public:
      void print()
      {
            cout<<"\nANSWER = "<<ans;
      }
};
```

```cpp
class Large3 : public AB, public res
{
 protected:
      int c;
 public:
      void read()
      {
           AB::read();
           cout<<"Enter C : ";
           cin>>c;
      }
      void putdata(int a,int b,int c)
      {
           AB::putdata(a,b);
           this->c = c;
      }
      void calculate()
      {
           ans=a>b?(a>c?a:b):(b>c?b:c);
      }
      void print()
      {
           AB::print();
           cout<<"\nC = "<<c;
           res::print();
      }
};
void main()
{
      Large3 l1;
      l1.read();
      l1.calculate();
      l1.print();
}
```

6. Program to understand the concepts of hierarchy inheritance

```cpp
#include <iostream.h>
class Radius
{
 protected:
      float rad;
 public:
      void read()
      {
           cout<<"\nEnter radius: ";
           cin>>rad;
      }
      void print()
      {
           cout<<"\nRadius: "<<rad;
      }
};
```

```cpp
class Circle : public Radius
{
  private:
      float area;
      float circum;
  public:
      void read()
      {
          Radius::read();
      }
      void calculate()
      {
          area = 3.14 * rad * rad;
          circum = 2 * 3.14 * rad;
      }
      void print()
      {
          Radius::print();
          cout<<"\nCircle area: "<<area;
          cout<<"\nCircle circumference: "<<circum;
      }
};
class Sphere : public Radius
{
  private:
      float area;
      float vol;
  public:
      void read()
      {
          Radius::read();
      }
      void calculate()
      {
          area = 4 * 3.14 * rad * rad;
          vol = 4 / 3.0 * 3.14 * rad * rad * rad;
      }
      void print()
      {
          Radius::print();
          cout<<"\nSphere area: "<<area;
          cout<<"\nSphere volume: "<<vol;
      }
};
void main()
{
      Circle c1;
      Sphere s1;
      c1.read();
      s1.read();
      c1.calculate();
      s1.calculate();
      c1.print();
      s1.print();
}
```

8 ADVANCED AND DYNAMIC POLYMORPHISM PROGRAMS

1. Program to understand the concepts of constructors & destructor in derived class

```cpp
// Program 1
#include <iostream.h>
class A
{
  protected:
      int a;
  public:
      A()
      {
            cout<<"\nHai from Class - A()\n";
            a = 0;
      }
      A(int a)
      {
            cout<<"\nHai from Class - A(int)\n";
            putdata(a);
      }
      ~A()
      {
            cout<<"\nBye from Class - A()\n";
      }
      void putdata(int a)
      {
            this->a = a;
      }
      void print()
      {
            cout<<"\nA = "<<a;
      }
};
class B
{
  protected:
      int b;
```

```cpp
    public:
        B()
        {
            cout<<"\nHai from Class - B()\n";
            b = 0;
        }
        B(int b)
        {
            cout<<"\nHai from Class - B(int)\n";
            putdata(b);
        }
        ~B()
        {
            cout<<"\nBye from Class - B()\n";
        }
        void putdata(int b)
        {
            this->b = b;
        }
        void print()
        {
            cout<<"\nB = "<<b;
        }
};
class AB : public A, public B
{
  public:
        AB()
        {
            cout<<"\nHai from Class - AB()\n";
        }
        AB(int a,int b) : A(a), B(b)
        {
            cout<<"\nHai from Class - AB(int,int)\n";
        }
        ~AB()
        {
            cout<<"\nBye from Class - AB()\n";
        }
        void putdata(int a,int b)
        {
            A::putdata(a);
            B::putdata(b);
        }
        void print()
        {
            A::print();
            B::print();
        }
};
void main() {
    AB a1,a2(1234,4321);
    a1.print();
    a2.print();
}
```

```
// Program 2
#include <iostream.h>
#include <string.h>
class stud
{
 protected:
      int rollno;
      char name[30];
 public:
      stud()
      {
            rollno=0;
            strcpy(name,"");
      }
      stud(int r,char n[])
      {
            rollno=r;
            strcpy(name,n);
      }
      void read()
      {
            cout<<"\nEnter Roll Number and Name\n";
            cin>>rollno>>name;
      }
      void print()
      {
            cout<<"\nRoll Number: "<<rollno;
            cout<<"\nName: "<<name;
      }
};
class test : public stud
{
 protected:
      int regno;
 public:
      test()
      {
            regno=0;
      }
      test(int r1,char n[],int r2) : stud(r1,n)
      {
            regno=r2;
      }
      void read()
      {
            stud::read();
            cout<<"Enter Register Number: ";
            cin>>regno;
      }
      void print() {
            stud::print();
            cout<<"\nRegister Number: "<<regno;
      }
};
```

```
void main()
{
    test t1(100,"Bjarne Stroustrup",12345),t2;
    t2.read();
    t1.print();
    t2.print();
}
```

2. Program to understand the concepts of virtual base class

```
#include <iostream.h>
class Employee
{
  protected:
    int no;
    char name[30];
  public:
    void read()
    {
        cout<<"\nEnter Employee Number: ";
        cin>>no;
        cout<<"\nEnter Employee Name: ";
        cin>>name;
    }
    void print()
    {
        cout<<"\nEmployee Number: "<<no;
        cout<<"\nEmployee Name: "<<name;
    }
};
class RegularSalary : virtual public Employee
{
  protected:
    float basic_pay;
    float da;
    float hra;
    float tot_reduction;
    float net1;
  public:
    void read()
    {
        cout<<"\nEnter Basic Pay : ";
        cin>>basic_pay;
        cout<<"\nEnter Dearness Allowance : ";
        cin>>da;
        cout<<"\nEnter House Rent Allowance : ";
        cin>>hra;
        cout<<"\nEnter Total Reduction : ";
        cin>>tot_reduction;
        net1 = (basic_pay + da + hra) - tot_reduction;
    }
```

```cpp
    void print() {
        cout<<"\nBasic Pay: "<<basic_pay;
        cout<<"\nDearness Allowance: "<<da;
        cout<<"\nHouse Rent Allowance: "<<hra;
        cout<<"\nTotal Reduction: "<<tot_reduction;
        cout<<"\nNet Regular Salary: "<<net1;
    }
};
class ExtraSalary : virtual public Employee
{
  protected:
    int hr_worked;
    float wages_per_hr;
    float net2;
  public:
    void read()
    {
        cout<<"\nEnter Number of Hours Worked: ";
        cin>>hr_worked;
        cout<<"\nEnter Wages Per Hour: ";
        cin>>wages_per_hr;
        net2 = hr_worked * wages_per_hr;
    }
    void print() {
        cout<<"\nNumber of Hours Worked: "<<hr_worked;
        cout<<"\nWages Per Hour: "<<wages_per_hr;
        cout<<"\nNet Extra Salary: "<<net2;
    }
};
class TotalSalary : public RegularSalary, public ExtraSalary
{
  protected:
    float salary;
  public:
    void read()
    {
        Employee::read();
        RegularSalary::read();
        ExtraSalary::read();
        salary = net1 + net2;
    }
    void print() {
        Employee::print();
        RegularSalary::print();
        ExtraSalary::print();
        cout<<"\nTotal Salary: "<<salary;
    }
};
void main()
{
    TotalSalary e1;
    e1.read();
    e1.print();
}
```

3. Prerequisite program to understand the concepts of virtual function

```cpp
#include <iostream.h>
class base
{
  public:
      void display()
      {
            cout<<"\nBase Class";
      }
};
class derived : public base
{
  public:
      void display()
      {
            cout<<"\nDerived Class";
      }
};
void main()
{
      base b1,*bp;
      derived d1,*dp;
      bp = &b1;
      bp->display();
      bp = &d1;
      bp->display();
      dp = &d1;
      dp->display();
      //dp = &b1;
      //dp->display();
}
```

4. Program to understand the concepts of virtual function

```cpp
#include <iostream.h>
class base
{
  public:
      virtual void display()
      {
            cout<<"\nBase Class";
      }
};
class derived : public base
{
  public:
      void display()
      {
            cout<<"\nDerived Class";
      }
};
```

```
void main()
{
    base b1,*bp;
    derived d1,*dp;
    bp = &b1;
    bp->display();
    bp = &d1;
    bp->display();
    dp = &d1;
    dp->display();
    //dp = &b1;
    //dp->display();
}
```

5. Program to understand the concepts of abstract and pure virtual function

```
#include <iostream.h>
class circle
{
  protected:
      float rad;
      float ans;
  public:
      virtual void calculate()=0; //pure virtual
      void read()
      {
          cout<<"Enter Radius = ";
          cin>>rad;
      }
      void print()
      {
          cout<<"\nRadius = "<<rad;
          cout<<"\nResult = "<<ans;
      }
};
class area : public circle
{
  public:
      void calculate()
      {
          ans=3.14*rad*rad;
      }
};
class circum : public circle
{
  public:
      void calculate()
      {
          ans=2*3.14*rad;
      }
};
```

```cpp
void main()
{
    circle *cp;
    // circle c1; abstract class
    area a1;
    circum c1;
    int choice;
    do
    {
        cout<<"\n\n1. Calculate Circle Area";
        cout<<"\n2. Calculate Circle Circumference";
        cout<<"\n3. Exit";
        cout<<"\n\nEnter Choice : ";
        cin>>choice;
        if(choice==1)
            cp = &a1;
        else if(choice==2)
            cp = &c1;
        else if(choice==3)
            break;
        else
        {
            cout<<"\n\nInvalid Choice";
            continue;
        }
        cp->read();
        cp->calculate();
        cp->print();
    }while(1);
}
```

9 FORMATTED & UNFORMATTED I/O PROGRAMS

1. Program to understand the concepts of unformatted I/O

```
// Program 1
#include <iostream.h>
void main()
{
    char ch;
    char str[30];
    int i=123,j=321;
    cout<<"Enter Character : ";
    ch = cin.get();
    cout<<"\nGiven Character ";
    cout.put(ch);
    cin.get();
    cout<<"\nEnter String : ";
    cin.getline(str,10);
    cout<<"\nGiven String is ";
    cout.write(str,5);
    cout<<"\n"<<i<<" "<<j;
}

// Program 2
#include <iostream.h>
#include <string.h>
void main()
{
    char str[30]="Bjarne Stroustrup";
    int i;
    for(i=0;i<=strlen(str);i++)
    {
        cout.write(str,i);
        cout<<"\n";
    }
    for(i=strlen(str)-1;i>=0;i--)
    {
        cout.write(str,i);
        cout<<"\n";
    }
}
```

2. Program to understand the concepts of formatted I/O

```cpp
// Program 1
#include <iostream.h>
void main()
{
    int i=123,j=4567;
    cout<<endl;
    cout.width(10);
    cout<<i;
    cout.width(10);
    cout<<j;
}
```

```cpp
// Program 2
#include <iostream.h>
void main()
{
    int i=123,j=4567;
    cout<<endl;
    cout.fill('*');
    cout.width(10);
    cout<<i<<endl;
    cout.width(10);
    cout<<j;
}
```

```cpp
// Program 3
#include <iostream.h>
void main()
{
    float a=12.34,b=567.89;
    cout.setf(ios::showpoint);
    cout.precision(3);
    cout<<endl;
    cout.width(10);
    cout<<a;
    cout.width(10);
    cout<<b;
}
```

```cpp
// Program 4
#include <iostream.h>
void main()
{
    int c=123,d=-321;
    cout.fill('*');
    cout.setf(ios::internal,ios::adjustfield);
    cout<<endl;
    cout.width(10);
    cout<<c<<endl;
    cout.width(10);
    cout<<d;
    cout.setf(ios::left,ios::adjustfield);
    cout<<endl;
```

```
        cout.width(10);
        cout<<c<<endl;
        cout.width(10);
        cout<<d;
        cout.setf(ios::right,ios::adjustfield);
        cout<<endl;
        cout.width(10);
        cout<<c<<endl;
        cout.width(10);
        cout<<d;
}

// Program 5
#include <iostream.h>
void main()
{
        float c=12.34,d=-.43210;
        cout.setf(ios::uppercase);
        cout.setf(ios::scientific,ios::floatfield);
        cout<<endl;
        cout.width(20);
        cout<<c;
        cout.width(20);
        cout<<d;
        cout.setf(ios::fixed,ios::floatfield);
        cout<<endl;
        cout.width(20);
        cout<<c;
        cout.width(20);
        cout<<d;
}

// Program 6
#include <iostream.h>
void main()
{
        int c=123,d=-321;
        cout.setf(ios::showpos);
        cout.setf(ios::dec,ios::basefield);
        cout<<endl;
        cout.width(20);
        cout<<c;
        cout.width(20);
        cout<<d;
        cout.setf(ios::oct,ios::basefield);
        cout<<endl;
        cout.width(20);
        cout<<c;
        cout.width(20);
        cout<<d;
        cout.setf(ios::uppercase);
        cout.setf(ios::hex,ios::basefield);
        cout<<endl;
        cout.width(20);
        cout<<c;
```

```
        cout.width(20);
        cout<<d;
        cout.unsetf(ios::uppercase);
        cout<<endl;
        cout.width(20);
        cout<<c;
        cout.width(20);
        cout<<d;
}
```

3. Program to understand the concepts of formatted I/O using manipulators

```
#include <iostream.h>
#include <iomanip.h>
void main()
{
        float x=123.45;
        int y = 123;
        cout<<setiosflags(ios::showpoint);
        cout<<setprecision(3)<<setfill('*');
        cout<<endl<<setw(10)<<x<<endl;
        cout<<resetiosflags(ios::showpoint);
        cout<<endl<<setw(10)<<x<<endl;
        cout<<setiosflags(ios::showbase);
        cout<<setiosflags(ios::hex);
        cout<<endl<<setw(10)<<y<<endl;
        cout<<resetiosflags(ios::showbase);
        cout<<endl<<setw(10)<<y<<endl;
}
```

10 FILE HANDLING PROGRAMS

1. Program to understand the concepts of file writing

```
// Program 1
#include <fstream.h>
void main()
{
    ofstream outfile;
    outfile.open("cppexpert.dat");
    outfile<<"Bjarne Stroustrup\n";
    outfile.close();
}

// Program 2
#include <fstream.h>
void main()
{
    fstream outfile("cppexpert.dat",ios::out);
    outfile<<"Bjarne Stroustrup\n";
    outfile.close();
}

// Program 3
#include <fstream.h>
void main()
{
    fstream outfile("cppexpert.dat",ios::app);
    outfile<<"Bjarne Stroustrup\n";
    outfile.close();
}
```

2. Program to read the specified file contents

```
#include <fstream.h>
void main()
{
    char fn[30];
    ifstream infile;
    char ch;
```

```
        cout<<"\nEnter file name: ";
        cin>>fn;
        infile.open(fn);
        if(infile.fail())
        {
            cout<<"\nFile not found";
            return;
        }
        do
        {
            ch = infile.get();
            cout<<ch;
        } while(!infile.eof());
        infile.close();
}
```

3. Program to calculate the sum and average of numbers from val.dat file. The contents of val.dat is

```
        10
        45
        78
        ...
```

```
#include <fstream.h>
void main()
{
        fstream infile("val.dat",ios::in);
        int x,sum=0,n=0;
        float avg;
        if(infile.fail())
        {
            cout<<"\nFile not found";
            return;
        }
        do
        {
            infile>>x;
            if(infile.eof())
                    break;
            cout<<endl<<x;
            sum+=x;
            n++;
        } while(1);
        avg = sum / (float)n;
        cout<<endl<<"N = "<<n;
        cout<<endl<<"Sum = "<<sum;
        cout<<endl<<"Average = "<<avg;
}
```

4. Program to understand the concepts of binary file writing and reading

```cpp
#include <fstream.h>
void main() {
    fstream inoutfile;
    char a;
    int b;
    float c;
    double d;
    inoutfile.open("test.bin",ios::binary|ios::out);
    a = 'A';
    b = 123;
    c = 1.23;
    d = 12.3;
    inoutfile.write(&a, sizeof(a));
    inoutfile.write((char*)&b, sizeof(b));
    inoutfile.write((char*)&c, sizeof(c));
    inoutfile.write((char*)&d, sizeof(d));
    inoutfile.close();
    inoutfile.open("test.bin",ios::binary|ios::in);
    if(inoutfile.fail()) {
        cout<<"\nFile not found";
        return;
    }
    inoutfile.read(&a, sizeof(a));
    inoutfile.read((char*)&b, sizeof(b));
    inoutfile.read((char*)&c, sizeof(c));
    inoutfile.read((char*)&d, sizeof(d));
    cout<<"\nA = "<<a;
    cout<<"\nB = "<<b;
    cout<<"\nC = "<<c;
    cout<<"\nD = "<<d;
    inoutfile.close();
}
```

5. Program to understand the concepts of random access file handling. The contents of alpha.dat is abcdefghijkl.....

```cpp
#include <fstream.h>
void main() {
    ifstream infile("alpha.dat");
    char c;
    int i=0;
    while(!infile.eof()) {
        infile.seekg(i,ios::cur);
        c = infile.get();
        cout<<endl<<c;
        i = i + 2;
    }
    infile.seekg(0,ios::beg);
    cout<<endl<<infile.tellg();
    infile.seekg(0,ios::end);
    cout<<"\nFile Size: "<<infile.tellg();
    infile.close();
}
```

72

6. Program to understand the concepts of command line arguments

```
#include <iostream.h>
void main(int argc,char *argv[])
{
    int i;
    cout<<"Number of Argument is "<<argc;
    for(i=0;i<argc;i++)
        cout<<endl<<argv[i];
}
```

7. Program to read the specified file contents using command line arguments

```
#include <fstream.h>
void main(int argc,char *argv[])
{
    ifstream infile;
    char ch;
    if(argc!=2)
    {
        cout<<"\nUsage: FREAD <file_name>";
        return;
    }
    infile.open(argv[1]);
    if(infile.fail())
    {
        cout<<"\nThe file "<<argv[1]<<" is not found";
        return;
    }
    do
    {
        ch = infile.get();
        cout<<ch;
    } while(!infile.eof());
    infile.close();
}
```

11 TEMPLATE PROGRAMS

1. Prerequisite program to understand the concepts of function template

```
#include <iostream.h>
void swap(int &x,int &y)
{
    int t;
    t = x;
    x = y;
    y = t;
}
void main()
{
    int a,b;
    cout<<"\nEnter A and B values\n";
    cin>>a>>b;
    cout<<"\nBefore, calling function";
    cout<<"\nA = "<<a<<"\nB = "<<b;
    swap(a,b);
    cout<<"\nAfter, calling function";
    cout<<"\nA = "<<a<<"\nB = "<<b;
}
```

2. Program to understand the concepts of function template

```
#include <iostream.h>
template <class T>
void swap(T &x,T &y)
{
    T t;
    t = x;
    x = y;
    y = t;
}
void main()
{
    int a,b;
    float c,d;
    cout<<"\nEnter A and B values\n";
```

```
        cin>>a>>b;
        cout<<"\nBefore, calling function";
        cout<<"\nA = "<<a<<"\nB = "<<b;
        swap(a,b);
        cout<<"\nAfter, calling function";
        cout<<"\nA = "<<a<<"\nB = "<<b;
        cout<<"\nEnter C and D values\n";
        cin>>c>>d;
        cout<<"\nBefore, calling function";
        cout<<"\nC = "<<c<<"\nD = "<<d;
        swap(c,d);
        cout<<"\nAfter, calling function";
        cout<<"\nC = "<<c<<"\nD = "<<d;
}
```

3. Program to understand the concepts of class template

```
#include <iostream.h>
template <class T>
class Large2
{
  private:
      T a;
      T b;
  public:
      void read()
      {
          cout<<"\nEnter two numbers\n";
          cin>>a>>b;
      }
      void print()
      {
          cout<<"\nA = "<<a;
          cout<<"\nB = "<<b;
          cout<<"\nLarge = "<<(a>b?a:b);
      }
};
template <class T1, class T2>
class Small2
{
  private:
      T1 a;
      T2 b;
  public:
      void read() {
          cout<<"\nEnter two numbers\n";
          cin>>a>>b;
      }
      void print() {
          cout<<"\nA = "<<a;
          cout<<"\nB = "<<b;
          cout<<"\nSmall = "<<(a<b?a:b);
      }
};
```

```
void main()
{
  Large2 <int> l1;
  Large2 <float> l2;
  Large2 <double> l3;
  Large2 <char> l4;
  Small2 <int, int> s1;
  Small2 <int, float> s2;
  Small2 <float, int> s3;
  Small2 <float, float> s4;
  Small2 <double, double> s5;
  l1.read();
  l1.print();
  l2.read();
  l2.print();
  l3.read();
  l3.print();
  l4.read();
  l4.print();
  s1.read();
  s1.print();
  s2.read();
  s2.print();
  s3.read();
  s3.print();
  s4.read();
  s4.print();
  s5.read();
  s5.print();
}
```

12 MISCELLANEOUS PROGRAMS

1. Program to understand the concepts of accessing global variable

```cpp
#include<iostream.h>
int a = 100;
void main() {
  int a = 10;
  cout<<"\nA = "<<a;
  cout<<"\nA = "<<::a;
}
```

2. Prerequisite program to understand the concepts this keyword

```cpp
#include <iostream.h>
class A {
  private:
      int a;
  public:
      void read()
      {
          cout<<"\nEnter A Value: ";
          cin>>a;
      }
      void print()
      {
          cout<<"\nA = "<<a;
      }
      void putdata(int a)
      {
          a = a;
      }
};
void main() {
  A a1;
  a1.read();
  a1.print();
  a1.putdata(12345);
  a1.print();
}
```

3. Program to understand the concepts of this keyword

```
#include <iostream.h>
class A
{
  private:
      int a;
  public:
      void read()
      {
          cout<<"\nEnter A Value: ";
          cin>>a;
      }
      void print()
      {
          cout<<"\nA = "<<a;
      }
      void putdata(int a)
      {
          this->a = a;
      }
};
void main()
{
  A a1;
  a1.read();
  a1.print();
  a1.putdata(12345);
  a1.print();
}
```

4. Program to understand the concepts of calling base class method from derived class object

```
#include <iostream.h>
class stud
{
  protected:
      int regno;
      char name[30];
  public:
      void read()
      {
          cout<<"\nEnter Register Number: ";
          cin>>regno;
          cout<<"\nEnter Name: ";
          cin>>name;
      }
      void print()
      {
          cout<<"\nRegister Number: "<<regno;
          cout<<"\nName: "<<name;
      }
};
```

```
class personal_info : public stud
{
  private:
      char addr[70];
      char place[30];
  public:
      void read()
      {
          stud::read();
          cout<<"\nEnter Address: "; cin>>addr;
          cout<<"\nEnter Place: "; cin>>place;
      }
      void print()
      {
          stud::print();
          cout<<"\nAddress: "<<addr;
          cout<<"\nPlace: "<<place;
      }
};
void main()
{
      personal_info p1;
      p1.read();
      p1.print();
      p1.stud::print();
}
```

5. Program to understand the concepts of insertion and extraction operators overloading

```
#include <iostream.h>
class distance
{
  private:
      float feet;
      float inches;
  public:
      distance()
      {
          feet=0;
          inches=0;
      }
      void read()
      {
          cout<<"\nEnter Distance (Feet Inches)\n";
          cin>>feet>>inches;
      }
      void print()
      {
          cout<<"\nThe Distance is "<<feet<<"' "<<inches<<"\"\n";
      }
      friend ostream& operator << (ostream &out, const distance &d);
      friend istream& operator >> (istream &in, distance &d);
};
```

```
ostream& operator << (ostream &out, const distance &d)
{
    out<<"\nThe Distance is "<<d.feet<<"' "<<d.inches<<"\"\n";
    return out;
}
istream& operator >> (istream &in, distance &d)
{
    cout<<"\nEnter Distance (Feet Inches)\n";
    in>>d.feet>>d.inches;
    return in;
}
void main()
{
    distance d1,d2;
    cin>>d1;
    d2.read();
    d1.print();
    cout<<d2;
}
```

6. Program to understand the addition of members of two different classes using friend function

```
#include <iostream.h>
class dcm;
class dm
{
  private:
      float m;
  public:
      void read()
      {
          cout<<"\nEnter distance in metre: ";
          cin>>m;
      }
      void print()
      {
          cout<<"\nDistance in metres is "<<m<<"m\n";
      }
      friend dm add(dm,dcm);
      friend dcm add(dcm,dm);
};
class dcm
{
  private:
      float cm;
  public:
      void read()
      {
          cout<<"\nEnter distance in centi metre: ";
          cin>>cm;
      }
}
```

```
        void print()
        {
            cout<<"\nDistance in centi metres is "<<cm<<"cm\n";
        }
        friend dm add(dm,dcm);
        friend dcm add(dcm,dm);
};
dm add(dm d1,dcm d2)
{
        d1.m = d1.m + d2.cm / 100;
        return d1;
}
dcm add(dcm d1,dm d2)
{
        d1.cm = d1.cm + d2.m * 100;
        return d1;
}
void main()
{
        dm m1;
        dcm cm1;
        m1.read();
        cm1.read();
        m1.print();
        cm1.print();
        m1=add(m1,cm1);
        cm1=add(cm1,m1);
        m1.print();
        cm1.print();
}
```

7. Program to create the complete complex class

```
#include <iostream.h>
#include <math.h>
class complex
{
  private:
        float real;
        float img;
  public:
        complex(float r=0,float i=0)
        {
            putdata(r,i);
        }
        void read()
        {
            cout<<"\nEnter Complex Number (Real, Img)\n";
            cin>>real>>img;
        }
```

```
void print()
{
    cout<<"\nThe Complex Number is "<<real;
    if(img>=0)
        cout<<"+";
    cout<<img<<"i";
}
float getreal()
{
    return real;
}
float getimg()
{
    return img;
}
void conjugate()
{
    img = -img;
}
void putdata(float r=0,float i=0)
{
    real = r;
    img = i;
}
complex operator == (complex c)
{
    return real==c.real&&img==c.img ? 1 : 0;
}
complex operator != (complex c)
{
    return real!=c.real&&img!=c.img ? 1 : 0;
}
complex operator < (complex c)
{
    return real<c.real&&img<c.img ? 1 : 0;
}
complex operator <= (complex c)
{
    return real<=c.real&&img<=c.img ? 1 : 0;
}
complex operator > (complex c)
{
    return real>c.real&&img>c.img ? 1 : 0;
}
complex operator >= (complex c)
{
    return real>=c.real&&img>=c.img ? 1 : 0;
}
complex operator + (complex c)
{
    return complex(real+c.real,img+c.img);
}
```

```cpp
        complex operator - (complex c)
        {
            return complex(real-c.real,img-c.img);
        }
        complex operator - ()
        {
            return complex(-real,-img);
        }
        complex operator ++ ()
        {
            return complex(++real,++img);
        }
        complex operator -- ()
        {
            return complex(--real,--img);
        }
        complex operator * (complex c)
        {
            float mag1 = sqrt(real*real+img*img);
            float mag2 = sqrt(c.real*c.real+c.img*c.img);
            float ang1 = atan(img/real);
            float ang2 = atan(c.img/c.real);
            mag1 *= mag2;
            ang1 += ang2;
            c.real = mag1 * cos(ang1);
            c.img = mag1 * sin(ang1);
            return c;
        }
        complex operator / (complex c)
        {
            float mag1 = sqrt(real*real+img*img);
            float mag2 = sqrt(c.real*c.real+c.img*c.img);
            float ang1 = atan(img/real);
            float ang2 = atan(c.img/c.real);
            mag1 /= mag2;
            ang1 -= ang2;
            c.real = mag1 * cos(ang1);
            c.img = mag1 * sin(ang1);
            return c;
        }
        friend ostream& operator << (ostream &out, complex &c);
        friend istream& operator >> (istream &in, complex &c);
};
ostream& operator << (ostream &out, complex &c)
{
    c.print();
    return out;
}
istream& operator >> (istream &in, complex &c)
{
    c.read();
    return in;
}
```

```
void main()
{
    complex c1,c2,c3;
    cin>>c1>>c2;
    c3=c1+c2;
    cout<<c3;
    c1 = -c2;
    cout<<c1<<c2;
    c2 = ++c1;
    cout<<c1<<c2;
    c3 = c1 * c2;
    cout<<c1<<c2<<c3;
    c3 = c1 / c2;
    cout<<c1<<c2<<c3;
}
```

APPENDIX–HOW TO INSTALL TURBO C++: COMPILE&RUN A C++ PROGRAM

The first thing you need to understand is that computer (Machine) can only understand Machine language (Stream of 0s and 1s). In order to convert your C program source code to Machine code, you need to compile it. The compiler is the one, which converts source code to Machine code. In simple terms, you can understand that a compiler converts the human readable code to a machine readable format.

A1.1 Install Turbo C++

Download Turbo C++ for Windows. After download, install the Turbo C++ in the location D:\tcplus.

A1.2 Compile & Run a C++ Program

Step 1: Locate the TC.exe file and open it. You will find it at location D:\TCPLUS\BIN\.

Step 2: File > New (as shown in below picture) and then write your C++ program

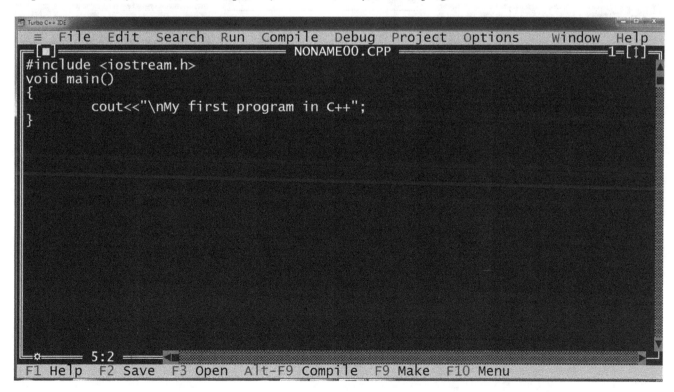

Step 3: Save the program using F2 (OR file > Save), remember the extension should be ".cpp". In the below screenshot I have given the name as first.cpp.

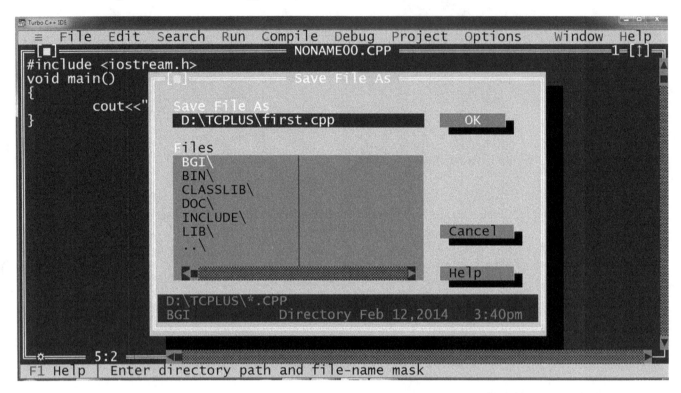

Step 4: Compile the program using Alt + F9 OR Compile > Compile (as shown in the below screenshot).

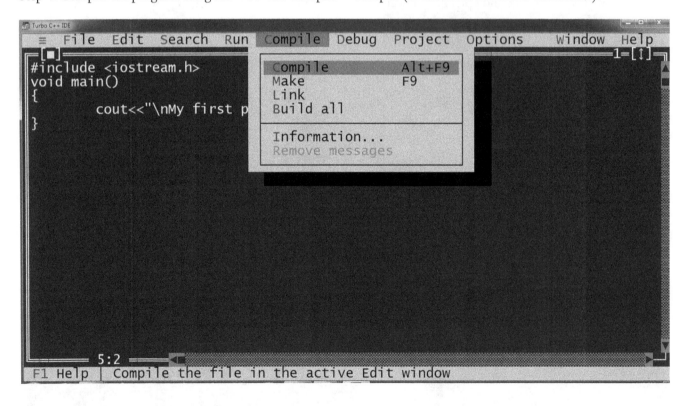

Step 5: Press Ctrl + F9 to Run (or select Run > Run in menu bar) the C++ program.

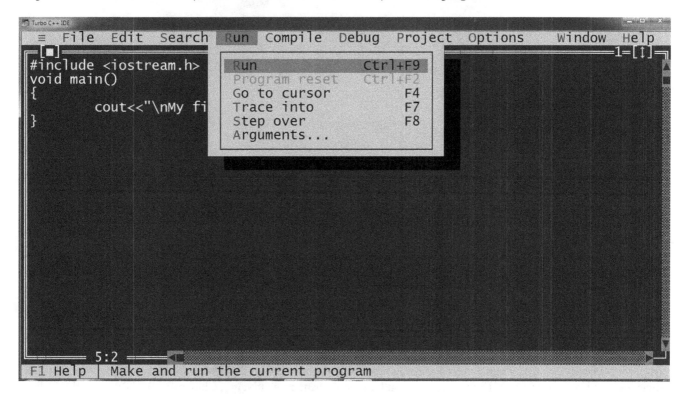

Step 6: Alt+F5 to view the output of the program on the output screen.

ABOUT THE AUTHOR

S.Anbazhagan was born in Mayiladuthurai, Tamil Nadu, India, on December 30, 1979. He received the Diploma in Computer Technology from Muthiah Polytechnic College, Annamalai Nagar, Chidambaram, Tamil Nadu, India, in 1997. He obtained his B.E. degree in Electrical Engineering in 2002, Post-Graduate Diploma in Computer Applications in 2004, M.E. degree in Computer Science and Engineering in 2009, and the Ph.D. degree in Computer Science and Engineering in 2015 from Annamalai University, Annamalai Nagar, Chidambaram, Tamil Nadu, India.

At present, he is an Assistant Professor in the Department of Electrical Engineering, Faculty of Engineering and Technology, Annamalai University, Annamalai Nagar, Chidambaram, India. He has published papers in 9 internationally reviewed journals and he has presented 6 international conference papers. He also authored book on Practice Guidebook for C Programming Language. His current research interests include computer programming languages, image processing, and soft computing techniques applied to various engineering problem domains.

Mr.S.Anbazhagan is an Associate of The Institution of Engineers (India) and a life member of the Indian Society of Technical Education. He received the best paper award at the IET-U.K. (formerly IEE) international conference in 2011. He appeared for GATE in 2009 and secured 87.77 percentile score. Also, he is a reviewer for the International Journal of Electrical Power & Energy Systems, Energy Conversion and Management, IET Generation, Transmission & Distribution, IEEE Transactions on Neural Networks and Learning Systems, IEEE Transactions on Power Systems, IEEE Transactions on Smart Grid and other international reputed journals.

www.ingramcontent.com/pod-product-compliance
Lightning Source LLC
Chambersburg PA
CBHW060202060326

40690CB00018B/4213